Forget-Me-Not, Iran

Forget-Me-Not, Iran
The Story of Keith Ransom-Kehler

Sarah Munro

intellect Bristol, UK / Chicago, USA

First published in the UK in 2011 by
Intellect, The Mill, Parnall Road, Fishponds, Bristol, BS16 3JG, UK

Copyright © 2011 Intellect Ltd

All rights reserved. No part of this publication may be reproduced, stored in a retrieval system, or transmitted, in any form or by any means, electronic, mechanical, photocopying, recording, or otherwise, without written permission.

A catalogue record for this book is available from the British Library.

Cover designer: Holly Rose
Copy-editor: Ed Hatton
Typesetting: Mac Style, Beverley, E. Yorkshire

ISBN 978-1-84150-411-7

Contents

A Letter to Keith	7
Preface	9
Introduction	11
'Forget-Me-Not, Iran': The Story of Keith Ransom-Kehler	39

A Letter to Keith

by Roger White

Why did you do it, Keith,
And you a looker?
Not your usual religious dame
in need of a good dentist
and a fitted bra.
Not one of those skinny ones
who make it their painful duty to love mankind
and purse their lips a lot
to let you know it isn't easy.
Not one of those.
Sharp dresser, too.
And brainy.
Not every man's kind of woman
but a looker.
And a real good talker, too.
It makes no sense, Keith.
You could have put your passion to another use.

We grow them odd here in Michigan,
but you were an odd one, even for us –
why, just your name, for starters.
And all your mooning about the library,
reading too much,
making little notes in little books. And your preaching.
I suppose your life was full enough
but your interest in God – was that normal?
We always said you could pray the paint off a barn door

Forget-Me-Not, Iran

at twenty paces, but we meant no harm.
It was as though you were always looking for something
you hadn't found.

And gallivanting around the world like you did,
visiting the Maoris and savages like that,
which we had only ever seen in *National Geographic*.
In those days we thought we were doing pretty good
if we made a trip to Chicago.
Nobody faulted you for going to the Holy Land,
you always were the studious kind
and they've got a helluva lot of religion there.

We heard you were sent on a special mission
to fight for a good cause.
Well, you'd be just the girl for that;
but why Persia, Keith?
Life still isn't worth a nickel there
and what do they know about plumbing?
With a tongue like yours, I'll bet you told
those folks a thing or two.
And when word got back that you had died
there's some as said
you'd found what you wanted at last.
I'm one who thinks you did, Keith,
who thinks you did.

All these years later
standing at the marker they put up for you here at home
and reading those words
and listening to what these decent people are saying
about you being a glorious martyr and all –
I'm bawling,
me a grown man,
three sons and a wife in the grave
and not what you call sentimental.

Why did you do it, Keith,
and you a looker?

(From *Another Song, Another Season*)

Preface

Robert Weinberg

In a small, well-loved collection of spiritual aphorisms entitled *The Hidden Words*, an intriguing verse inverts what might be our obvious human perception of, and response to, the occurrence of events contrary to our wishes. "My calamity is My providence," writes Bahá'u'lláh (1817–1892), the Prophet-Founder of the Bahá'í Faith, "outwardly it is fire and vengeance, but inwardly it is light and mercy."

Facing hardship, enduring pain, losing all – such things are a bitter pill to swallow for anyone. For those devoted to the life of the spirit, cruel misfortune – even violent opposition – are familiar stages of the journey of life. Walking a spiritual path in a material world is rarely an easy expedition. But, obedience to the object of her devotion certainly provided Keith Ransom-Kehler with her greatest human challenge and spiritual victory. Her courageous, albeit largely unknown, contribution to history is the subject of this play.

Those who knew Keith as a person of refinement, of exquisite taste for the beautiful things of this world, could never imagine that she would die alone, thousands of miles away from home, disappointed. She had gone to Persia to present an appeal to the Shah to alleviate the increasing measures being taken to suppress the Bahá'í Faith there, including a ban on Bahá'í literature entering the country and being printed and distributed.

To outward seeming, her mission – like that of Persia's Bábí and Bahá'í martyrs and heroes who had gone before her – was a failure. Yet, seeing the providence in the calamity of her untimely demise, Shoghi Effendi hailed her as an "intrepid defender and illustrious herald of God's Cause" and extolled her "magnificent deeds".

"Whatsoever occurreth in the world of being is light for His loved ones and fire for the people of sedition and strife," wrote Bahá'u'lláh. "Even if all the losses of the world were to be sustained by one of the friends of God, he would still profit thereby, whereas true loss would be borne by such as are wayward, ignorant and contemptuous." Although the author of the following saying had intended it otherwise, yet we find it pertinent to the operation of God's immutable Will: "Even or odd, thou shalt win the wager." "The friends of God shall win and profit under all conditions, and shall attain true wealth. In fire they remain cold, and from water they emerge dry. Their affairs are at variance with the affairs of men. Gain is their lot, whatever the deal. To this testifieth every wise one with a discerning eye, and every fair-minded one with a hearing ear."

In the same verse from *The Hidden Words* quoted at the outset, Bahá'u'lláh instructs the loved ones of God to rush towards such calamity: "Hasten thereunto that thou mayest become an eternal light and an immortal spirit." In this mystery lies the impetus that has motivated countless souls throughout the spiritual history of humanity to undertake magnificent and significant sacrificial deeds.

Keith Ransom-Kehler may have been reluctant in her haste towards calamity. Her efforts in worldly terms may have been in vain. But there is no doubt that her light and spirit will shine eternally, inspiring countless future generations, and that her story has fresh relevance today as the Bahá'ís of Iran continue to face virulent persecution and oppression.

Introduction

'Forget-Me-Not, Iran' was first performed at the UK Bahá'í Arts Academy in August 2008, brought into being through a team of actors, technicians and production hands, working voluntarily over many months. This play text is dedicated not only to Keith Ransom-Kehler herself, but also to those who first helped to bring her story alive, and those whom it has touched.

During 'Abdu'l-Bahá's[1] historic visit to London in 1911, he met an actor who asked Him to speak about 'the drama'. 'Abdu'l-Bahá replied, "*The drama is of the utmost importance. It has been a great educational power in the past and will be so again.*" He went on to recount that, as a child, He had seen a 'passion play' that affected Him so deeply He could not sleep for many nights. This is perhaps the 'power' He was referring to – the feeling of awe at witnessing, as if first-hand, *the spirit* of an experience, of seeing the effects of a great soul in action. And when this spirit moves the heart of those who witness it, it can have a profound effect.

It is heartening to learn that imagination is, in fact, one of the essential properties of our souls. 'Abdu'l-Bahá, in His Tablet to Dr Auguste Forel (a prominent psychiatrist of the late 19th and early 20th centuries) describes the relationship between this faculty of mind and the soul:

> Now regarding the question of whether the faculties of the mind and the human soul are one and the same. These faculties are but the inherent properties of the soul, such as the power of imagination, of thought, of understanding; powers that are the essential requisites of the reality of man, even as the solar ray is the inherent property of the sun.

The above passage implies that, by 'taking part' in a drama, even by simply being a member of an audience and thereby having our imagination stimulated, we can, in fact, be developing an aspect of our soul. Imagination is an essential tool that we need to use in order to feel a connection with the divine, to be able to feel the presence of that which exists beyond our material world. Therefore, one of the powers of drama may be its ability to stimulate the imagination and strengthen that connection.

The writings of the Guardian of the Bahá'í Faith[2] can also help us to understand the importance of drama within communities and the role that it can play in assisting others to come into contact with the power of Bahá'u'lláh's Teachings. Writing to an individual believer in 1932 regarding plays about the history and teachings of the Faith, he wrote:

> It is through such presentations that we can arouse the interest of the greatest number of peoples in the spirit of the Cause. That day will the Cause spread like wildfire when its spirit and teachings will be presented on the stage or in art and literature as a whole. Art can better awaken such noble sentiments than cold rationalizing, especially among the masses of the people.

Perhaps another aspect of the power of drama referred to by 'Abdu'l-Bahá is that theatre can reinforce the significance of historical events and the actions of individuals that helped to bring shape and form to Bahá'u'lláh's Teachings and develop the community being raised in His Name. In this way, the fabric holding together that community is enriched.

Since being inspired by the National Assembly of the Bahá'ís of the UK's invitation in 2002 to write poems, dramas or songs celebrating the life of Tahirih (the first woman believer in the new religion) for the 150th anniversary of her martyrdom, I have been writing and performing short dramas based on the lives of historical figures of the Bahá'í Faith. As an actor, it was feeling the power of bringing Tahirih alive to tell her own story in the small halls and living rooms where the short play was performed, and witnessing her sacrifice inspire and strengthen the faith of the Bahá'ís and their friends sitting in the audience, that encouraged me to continue with this type of service for the communities in which I have lived.

Forums such as the 'Bahá'í Arts Academy' (held in the United Kingdom since 1994), summer schools and conferences can really help to promote the creation of drama and the performing arts, as they provide a ready-made platform for performance and a receptive audience. I am eternally grateful to those who have helped create such opportunities by inviting dramatic contributions to their programs, and who have had faith in the power of dramatic art to stir and enrich the community.

I very much hope that this play text and its accompanying materials will be a small contribution to the growing pool of resources available to those who wish to arise and render the service of creating drama within their own communities. Most of all, I hope that it will awaken awareness of the spirit of Keith's sacrifice and, in doing so, perhaps even move some to render similarly heroic deeds in service to the Blessed Beauty.

Sarah Munro, October 2008

Introduction

Notes

1. 'Abdu'l-Bahá was the eldest son of Bahá'u'lláh, the Prophet-Founder of the Bahá'í Faith.
2. Shoghi Effendi became Guardian of the Bahá'í Faith in 1921 with the passing of his grandfather, 'Abdu'l-Bahá, and remained in that role until 1957 when he himself passed away. One of the functions of the Guardianship was to provide explanations of the Writings of both Bahá'u'lláh and 'Abdu'l-Bahá, as well as to guide the development of Bahá'í communities around the world.

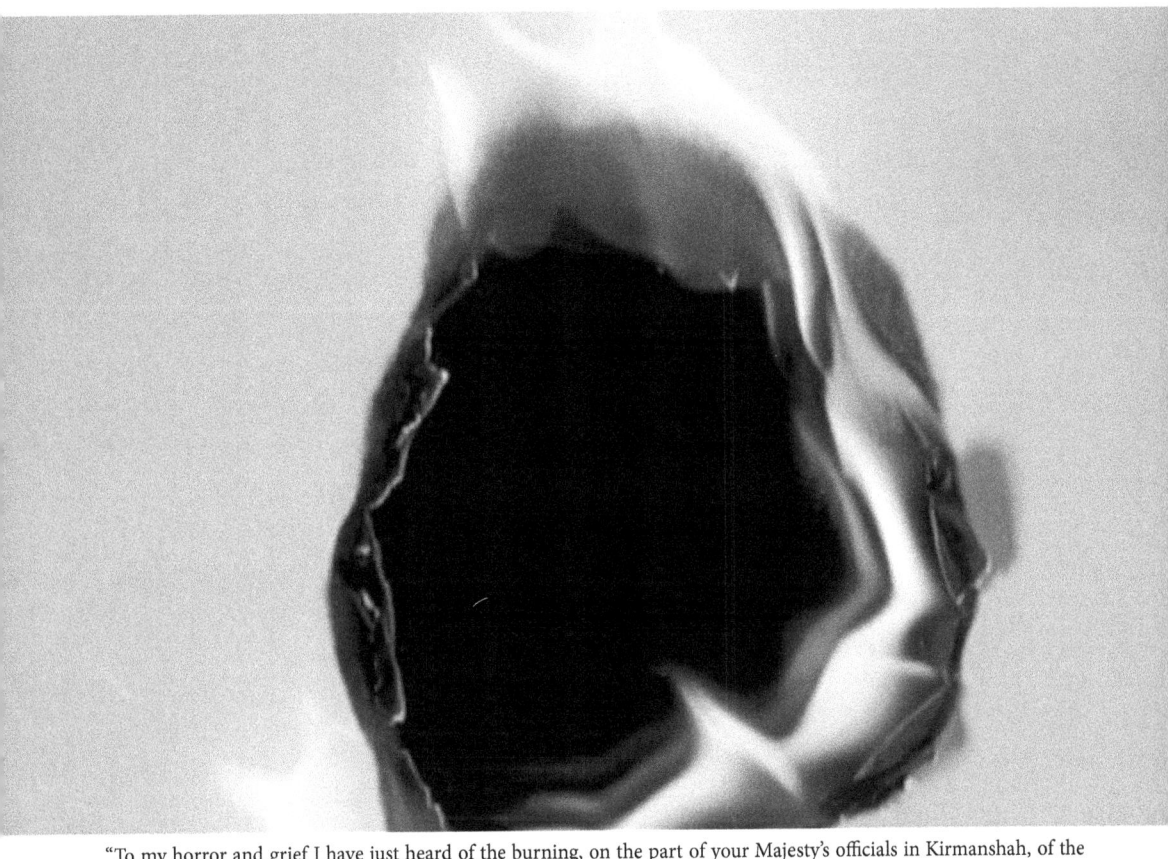

"To my horror and grief I have just heard of the burning, on the part of your Majesty's officials in Kirmanshah, of the sacred photographs of 'Abdu'l-Bahá."

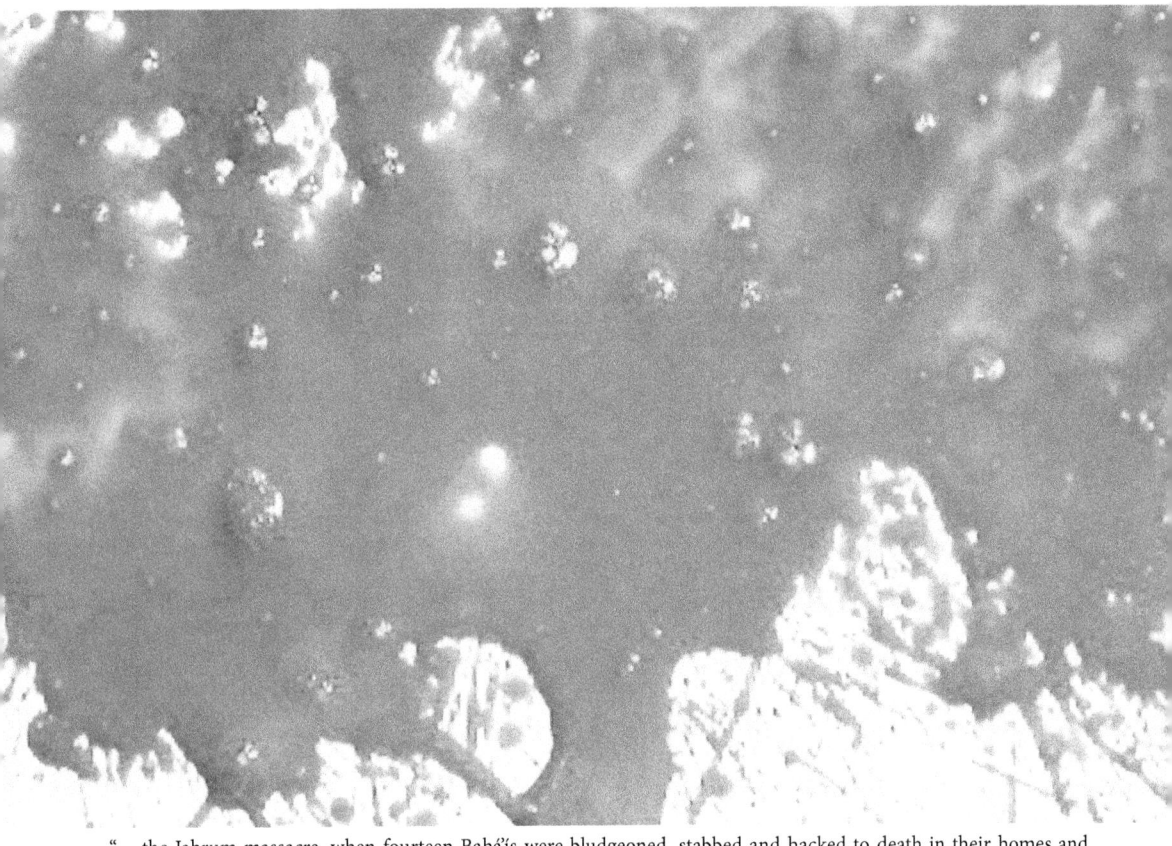
"... the Jahrum massacre, when fourteen Bahá'ís were bludgeoned, stabbed and hacked to death in their homes and streets."

"But this action causes him to topple over into the river, the weight of his armour pulling him down deep into the water."

"I have fallen, and am drowning, though I never faltered."

… "my tired old body fell, dragged down into the river by the weight of the task."

"Mine will be a very modest flower, perhaps like the single, tiny forget-me-not, watered by the blood of Quddús that I plucked from his graveside in Bárfurúsh…"

As used in the first production of 'Forget-me-Not, Iran', a clip from a short film of the Guardian of the Bahá'í Faith filmed at his home in Haifa, Palestine, circa 1950.

Sarah Munro played the role of Keith in the first performance of 'Forget-me-Not, Iran' at the Baháʼí UK Arts Academy, August 2008.

Sarah Munro as Keith in a still from Act One. Keith gives one of her infamous lectures.

Sarah Munro as Keith in a still from Act Two. Keith reminisces about her experiences meeting with the Bahá'í friends in Iran.

"Keith Ransom-Kehler, a highly intelligent, highly elegant, and highly opinionated young lady …"

"This photograph had been taken in Tehran only a few months before. Keith was beautifully dressed, facing the camera with elegant posture and a bright if somewhat tremulous smile. Just before the photo was taken, Keith had been weeping over the failure of her mission; she had held back the tears for the photographer."

Shoghi Effendi, Guardian of the Bahá'í Faith from 1921–1957. This picture was taken circa 1922 shortly after assuming the role of Guardianship.

Shoghi Effendi, Guardian of the Bahá'í Faith from 1921–1957.

'Forget-Me-Not, Iran':

The Story of Keith Ransom-Kehler

A Play in Two Acts
Runs at 55 minutes

Cast List:

Keith Ransom-Kehler – *American female*

Chairman of the National Spiritual Assembly of the Bahá'ís of the United States of America/ Maori Chief/American Ambassador – *American male*

Mullah/Iranian Government Official – *Persian male*

Paperboy/Aide/Guide/Iranian Girl – *Persian female (young)*

Set:

Stage left there is a low table and chair for the Chairman. At the back, there is a large screen on which the images are projected.

ACT ONE:

Keith's Awakening and World Travels

Spotlight comes up on the CHAIRMAN. He is a mature and dignified gentleman, in his early 60s, dressed in a 1930's American suit. He speaks to the audience throughout.

CHAIRMAN: It was in the winter of 1931, when I was serving as the Chairman of the National Spiritual Assembly of the Bahá'ís of the US and Canada that the Guardian, Shoghi Effendi, first asked our National Assembly to petition the Shah of Iran to allow the publication of Bahá'í literature in that country. This attempt failed, thwarted by political upheaval that took the Shah's attention away from our plea. Our second attempt was no more successful. We realised that powerful factions were what decided the occupation of his time and attention, not the Shah himself. We turned, lost and defeated back to Shoghi Effendi, knowing not what to do. He suggested that someone going there to meet with the Shah in person might achieve the mission. But who would that be?

Light snaps up on KEITH, dressed 'exceedingly elegantly'. She stands on stage right. Springing to life …

KEITH: Now, are there any questions? Yes, the lady with the beautiful blue wrap … Oh, that is *such* a lovely fabric! Is it Chanel? I thought so. Anyway, what was your question? *(she listens)* No, I'll be speaking about that subject tomorrow evening. It is then we will address the challenges of combining chicken-rearing with fruit farming, alright? It is an interesting subject indeed – I like to call it 'Fricken Farming'. Great for the economy and great for chickens. Since I was raised on a farm, I have been forever concerned with the depressing exigencies of these pitiable little creatures.

KEITH freezes.

CHAIRMAN: Keith Ransom-Kehler, a highly intelligent, highly elegant, and highly opinionated young lady, met 'Abdu'l-Bahá in September 1911 while on a visit to London. She was one of the seekers who flocked to hear Him speak. She wasn't a Bahá'í then, but became profoundly influenced by Him.

KEITH springs to life again.

KEITH: Yes, you sir, how can I help? *(she listens to his question – but he obviously says something that shocks her)* Sorry, let me just get this right. You are worried about the mental health of your daughter if you allow her to complete secondary school, because you actually believe that with more education, she'll have more to worry about in life … and what was the last bit? *(she listens while he repeats)* Oh yes, you think that women's lives should be simple – husband, motherhood and not to worry about the rest of the world.

Pause.

Well, sir, I just think that you have to get with the modern world. The equality of men and women is now a reality, and that means equality of education, first and foremost. Women's lives were not made to be simple. Women were made, sir, to bring solutions into this world, solutions to problems that men have created in large part. And if those women are going to find those solutions, those men are going to have to let them get educated. No! Scratch that. Women themselves, despite what small-minded and petty men like you think, have to get themselves educated. Do you think that by allowing your daughter an education that she will surpass you in intellect and show you up? Well – I think that she just will most likely do that. And more power to her. Good night.

She goes to exit, but then stops and turns back to the audience.

KEITH: My husband tells me I'm like a gun levelled at poor unsuspecting gentlemen *(with slight pity)* and he *(indicating the man she has just addressed)* obviously didn't know I was loaded.

She freezes.

CHAIRMAN: Ten years later, Keith became a Bahá'í in Chicago and plunged into the work – administration, organising community events and teaching. Then, in 1926, she went on pilgrimage …

A moving image of the Guardian is projected onto the screen which plays as she speaks.

KEITH: Meeting that majestic essence of purity, dear Shoghi Effendi … this youth under thirty, labouring day and night for us, sacrificing every human desire and tendency to further our efforts … with no more personal life than a graven image, no more thought of self than a breeze or a flower, just a hollow reed for the divine melody. Why! Any one of us is ready to die for him, but can we conscientiously number ourselves among those who are willing to live for him?

Being close to the Guardian in those days wasn't the only bounty on pilgrimage – of course, I also spent time with beloved Bahíyyih Khánum and Munírih Khánum, the Master's widow. Exquisite, fragrant, imperturbable, assured, they walk among the changing conditions of the world. They make no attempt to reform people, but ennoble them merely by their presence.

Oh! I didn't want to leave that place. Whoever does? But one day when I was overcome by this feeling of wishing to stay in heaven for the rest of my earthly life, dear Munírih Khánum came to me, held my hand and we looked into each other's eyes of sadness and said, "You should be very happy, for you have the opportunity to go out into the world and give to others these glad tidings."

She freezes.

CHAIRMAN: Keith left Haifa a firebrand, even more passionate, even more focussed and devoted than before. On the very night she arrived back in New York, she took the lead in a teaching campaign. For five consecutive days she lectured about the Bahá'í Faith in the ballroom of the Majestic Hotel to audiences of hundreds.

KEITH: Now we've come to the end of this series lectures … You have heard about Bahá'u'lláh, His healing Message, His wondrous Laws and Teachings. I would like to ask those of you who now consider yourself a Bahá'í to stay behind. The rest can leave. *(she turns away, waiting as people leave)*. Now, how many of you are there? *(she counts)* My! 35 souls! My dear friends, welcome, welcome to the Cause of God!

CHAIRMAN: Hearing of this groundbreaking success, the Guardian sent 35 ring stones as gifts.

A young PAPERBOY enters from the top of the auditorium.

PAPERBOY: Keith Ransom-Kehler! In our town for one night only!

There is a flash of light, as if KEITH is having her photograph taken. She poses. The flashes and poses continue between each of the PAPERBOY and CHAIRMAN's lines.

CHAIRMAN: For the next five years, Keith took many lecture and travel-teaching trips to cities all over the US.

PAPERBOY: Keith Ransom-Kehler! Speaker extraordinaire!

CHAIRMAN: On one particular campaign, she visited every Local Assembly from Washington to Los Angeles to instruct them on proper administrative functioning.

PAPERBOY: Intrepid world traveller! Passionate Bahá'í teacher! … Martyr!

Pause. PAPERBOY and CHAIR both sharply turn to look at KEITH.

CHAIRMAN: In 11 months, she gave 329 addresses. In Seattle alone, she gave 45 public talks.

PAPERBOY: *(wandering off stage)* Keith Ransom-Kehler – for one night only! Come and hear her speak …!

CHAIRMAN: Shoghi Effendi had given our National Assembly a special mission – to educate communities around the world on the pattern of Baháʼí administration. We needed to send a representative abroad. We sent Keith.

Keith's nine suitcases are pushed on from stage right.

CHAIRMAN: In June 1925, she set sail for Japan.

A loud foghorn sounds. Japanese music begins to play and the AIDE takes a red Japanese kimono out of the top suitcase, which KEITH slips luxuriantly into.

KEITH: On my third day, I was invited to a fashionable tea party given by Mrs Kuroda, the wife of a famous virtuoso. I was so charmed by the highly refined household and the elegant gathering. I wore a beautiful red silk kimono and just the most exquisite pearls you have ever seen! I was particularly charmed by Mrs Kuroda's 85-year-old mother. Though I did find it taxing having to return the deep bows with which everyone else effortlessly greeted me.

Music fades to off.

The next day, we met a Japanese Christian minister. I must say I was pleased when he remarked, "Between me and my next door neighbour there is a wall of formality, but I seem to have been friends with Mrs Keith for many years and yet I have just met her." Well, don't you just think that he needs to get over himself and go round to that neighbour and invite him over for tea or something. Neighbours should talk, for God's sake!

KEITH is helped out of the Japanese robe.

CHAIRMAN: Keith's next stop was China, sailing to Shanghai in August and then onto Guangzhou in the south …

The AIDE takes out a Chinese tea set and sets up 'chairs' and a 'table' using the suitcases. Meanwhile, KEITH goes to fetch the rest of the suitcases.

KEITH: So, Ling and Chan Liu, who became Baháʼís through dear Martha, met me off the boat. Ling was wearing the most delightful peach-coloured Chinese outfit for the occasion. It wasn't easy to transport my mountains of luggage to their house. As we got out of the taxi, rain just poured down and it was only then that I learnt there was no road. To reach their house, every piece of luggage would have to traverse two sets of railroad tracks, a golf course, a vacant lot, a deep ditch and an old fort. Ling and I dragged three pieces of luggage and went to get their servant while Chan looked after the rest. We practically swam the train tracks, the golf course, the vacant lot, the ditch and the old fort. I was embarrassed that they had to go all this trouble just for little ol' me. But, at last, everything was home and we all sat down to tea.

KEITH and the AIDE sip tea together.

There were signs everywhere that China was preparing for civil war. I was appalled by the poverty and hardship under which most people laboured. Oh! This aching body of man cries out for its new God-sent freedom. Chan Lui asked shyly if the Guardian had ever spoken about China. With what thrilling joy I was able to tell him that, Yes! On several occasions Shoghi Effendi has spoken of the great importance of the work in China.

The low sound of a didgeridoo is heard.

CHAIRMAN: The next stop for Keith was Australia. A long sea voyage lasting nearly a week was what it her took to get there.

KEITH: Oh! The ocean was a gorgeous lapis blue, the sky pale, the sunlight mellow, the clouds shining white, the breeze kind, while the screaming of the monkeys among the dense coconut thickets that crowded the water's edge created a pandemonium of meaningless energy. But everyone on the ship spoke only Japanese. I had no-one to talk to, no-one to dress up for. I ate alone … but I still always dressed for dinner. And then, I arrived!

The AIDE stands ready with a huge bunch of flowers that she has taken from one of the suitcases and hands it to KEITH.

I immediately began a hectic schedule of lectures and Baháʼí gatherings. Everywhere I spoke I was presented with beautifully arranged bouquets of flowers so that sometimes I seemed literally lost in a wilderness of colour and fragrance! I must say that my clothes were also much appreciated in frontier Australia. Women there just long for a little refinement and splendour! But it wasn't all roses.

KEITH hands the flowers back to the AIDE.

I had to minister to some tender egos while presenting the demanding standards of Bahá'í beliefs. Some people who serve on Bahá'í Assemblies are not really Bahá'ís at all – they have all sorts of reservations and other affiliations. Some even profess themselves to be Communists! The real Bahá'ís in Adelaide number themselves to about 5.

And, one evening in Newcastle near Sydney, I delivered an address to a room full of hecklers. At the back there was an officious-looking man with a dog. That filthy beast came to the platform, sniffed me and retired to its master's side. The whole scene resembled something out of *Huckleberry Finn*. There were interruptions, exclamations, comings and goings all through my talk. People rose and gave their own speeches during question time. The chairman finally said to them, "Make your questions brief," and then turned to me and said, "Make your answers brief." I replied, "I shall answer myself as adequately as possible to the question, sir." And proceeded to do so for another hour and a half.

KEITH freezes. The AIDE takes a piece of black lace out of a suitcase and assists KEITH to fix it over her hair.

CHAIRMAN: Keith's next adventure was in New Zealand, where she delighted in meeting the Maori people.

KEITH: I donned the traditional black lace of the natives and went to the village of Wacka. Chief Mita Taupokei had arranged the meeting. When I arrived, a little boy was sent to ring a bell through the streets and in they pressed – grandmothers, infants-in-arms, college students – all with great curiosity. The old Chief spoke an introduction in his native tongue. My guide translated …

The GUIDE comes forward and stands next to KEITH to translate, pausing between each sentence to 'listen' to the MAORI CHIEF.

MAORI CHIEF: *(played by the Chairman)* Ringa pakia a ka mate. Ka mate ka ura. Ka ura tene. Te tangata pu huru huru Mrs Ransom-Kehler.

GUIDE:	Welcome to Mrs Keith Ransom-Kehler! To what great matter are we about to listen? It must be a subject of such great importance as this stranger has travelled over many seas to share with the Maoris, an obscure and forgotten people. We await impatiently the unfolding of her news and message.
KEITH:	Sir Chief *(bowing in respect)*, I come to talk to you about unity in diversity and the value of the Maori culture from the Bahá'í viewpoint.
CHIEF:	Nana, tiki mai whaka whiti te ra a. Upane, kaupane upane, kaupane whiti te ra! Hu!
GUIDE:	*(interpreting the Chief)* Congratulations! Congratulations! You bring good news to our people. This is the first time that a white woman has ever come to speak to us. And the first time we have heard this Message of kindness and peace.

The AIDE steps back, taking the black lace that KEITH hands her, placing it on one of the suitcases before exiting. KEITH's mood changes again. She comes forward, forlorn, and sits heavily on a suitcase. As the CHAIR speaks, the spotlight on KEITH gradually narrows, until it is a sharp, cold light.

CHAIRMAN:	Then Keith took off back to the East, this time to Burma. It was a difficult voyage. She fell into an abyss of self-doubt, feeling her efforts were in vain. Having suffered a stillbirth before losing her husband only a few years before, the profound loneliness she often felt returned. Believing that the other passengers on the ship disliked her, Keith kept to herself, playing solitaire in the lounge for long hours.
KEITH:	*(staring up into the light)* Oh, Shoghi Effendi! I am bearing witness throughout the world to a light I cannot see. I read the prayers, try to meditate, wring my hands and cry aloud to heaven, but the skies are brass. Am I too small for God to know? ... But there stirs somewhere in the depths of my withered soul a faint assurance and protest – no! no! *(with more strength, standing)* As Ralph Waldo Emerson once said, "To be loved, one must be lovely." I must set to work on that. In obedience to 'Abdu'l-Bahá, I must attract people to myself for the sake of the Faith.

The light broadens out and becomes warm again. Her mood changes and becomes bright. Upbeat Indian music plays. KEITH lifts two suitcases and 'arrives' in India.

CHAIRMAN: After three exceedingly full weeks of engagements in Burma, Keith moved onto India.

KEITH: My arrival in Calcutta was less than thrilling. As I disembarked from the ship, I realised that there was no one to meet me. As usual, the only address I had was a post office box. So I had a coolie take my mountain of luggage ashore and sat waiting there for another half an hour. I was feeling rather forlorn so had summoned a taxi to take me to the nearest hotel, and was just climbing in, when a little man in a huge white turban asked me, "Are you Mrs Ransom-Kehler?" He introduced himself as Mr Pitram Singh, the secretary of the National Assembly of the Bahá'ís of India and Burma. He had such a beautiful, kind, gentle face, I couldn't be angry with him. It turned out there had been a mix-up about the time of the ship's docking.

During the next sequence, the AIDE rushes on with a sari, quickly dressing KEITH in it, the last piece being slung over her shoulder as KEITH delivers the line "I had arrived."

The next thing I knew a young man, holding a huge bunch of red roses rushed up to us shouting, "Welcome to India!" He was the chairman of the Local Assembly of Calcutta. I had arrived!

It was in India, addressing these huge gatherings of noisy, colourful people that I learned to ask in commanding tones from the podium: "Could all who feel bored, please leave." This always caused amusement and put me *en rapport* with the audience. These meetings tended to be kaleidoscopic – groups wandering in and out of the balcony, people talking all the way through, hawkers and paperboys shouting lustily outside the open windows, motor horns honking and the ceaseless din of the traffic.

She freezes, covering her ears, while the CHAIRMAN speaks.

CHAIRMAN: Keith's itinerary included Varanasi, Lucknow, Aligarh, Agra, New Delhi, Amritsar, Lahore, Karachi, Bombay, Hyderabad and Pune. All accompanied by the little man in the huge, white turban who had been instructed by the Guardian himself to do so.

KEITH: Oh! I was happy in India, but my stomach wasn't. I continued my tour through waves of sickness. I found the Bahá'ís in states of activity and inactivity. I had been instructed by the Guardian to 'reawaken' the Indian Bahá'ís. So I did that. After I gave the friends in Karachi a piece of my mind, someone apparently remarked, "We could feel the force and power coming out of you like a whip." Huh! So that's where my energy goes! In the Bombay community I was about as popular as income tax. But no matter how that lash of fire and light burned me, I would not complain and I would not let it go. I wasn't there to make friends.

Yet despite my unpopularity, I must have signed 10,000 autographs. Fame is indeed fickle. These "fans" of mine will always have to explain whose signature they have when they boast of it, unless the Guardian decides at some point to make me someone of significance.

The AIDE enters with a cable in her hand. Music off.

HELPER: Excuse me, Mrs Kehler.

KEITH: Yes, what is it, dear? You do know that I am having a rest-day today and do not wish to be disturbed?

HELPER: Yes, ma'am. But I have a telegram for you.

KEITH: A telegram? Why I'm not expecting one.

HELPER: It has your name at the top. It is from Haifa.

KEITH: Haifa? Well, what could this be?

She takes it, opens and silently reads it. The light narrows. Images of a woman drowning and of forget-me-nots float by on the screen.

KEITH: *(reading aloud)* "Feel urge request you proceed promptly Haifa preparatory extended summer tour Persia. Cherish high hopes your future services. Cable reply. Shoghi."

I am thunderstruck. In the first place, it has never seriously occurred to me that I was any part of the Guardian's plan. Of course he has written to me and has directed me only, I thought, because he didn't want to dampen my ardour and to encourage my volunteer effort. But to find I have entered into his scheme of things is … astonishing … and Persia? … I thought he had Europe in mind for me …

The AIDE puts the articles and objects into the suitcases and closes them, stacking them up behind KEITH who stands motionless and stunned.

KEITH: *(Turning to look at the prepared suitcases)* Well, the travel agents aren't open today so I can't book my steamer passage to Haifa now. Since it is my rest-day … I think I'll go to the movies.

KEITH exits. Ominous Eastern music begins quietly while CHAIR speaks.

CHAIRMAN: Thus, in a seemingly very low-key way, Keith began her life's crowning mission.

Stage lights off.

END OF ACT ONE

ACT TWO:

Persia

Ominous Eastern music plays louder. A red light lights the stage. The suitcases are taken off. Then images of blood are projected on the screen. KEITH enters and kneels stage right. The CHAIR enters and goes to his position. The music stops suddenly.

CHAIRMAN: A few years previously, the new Shah of Iran, Reza Pahlavi, had joined forces with the Mullahs against the Bahá'ís. The result was the Jahrum massacre, when fourteen Bahá'ís were bludgeoned, stabbed and hacked to death in their homes and streets. Twenty more were killed soon after in other towns.

A spotlight comes up on KEITH.

KEITH: This was only part of what I learned from Shoghi Effendi. He gave me books on Islam, which I stayed up all night reading. In my moments of terror, Bahíyyih Khánum would cup my chin and stroke my hand, chanting a prayer. She called me 'teacher'. On the day I left, she rose to her feet and enfolded me in her arms. "When you arrive in Persia," she told me, "give my love to every Bahá'í in that land, to the men and the women. And when you reach the holy city of Tehran, enter it in my name." This would be her last message to Persia.

KEITH exits.

CHAIRMAN: *(officially)* Mrs Keith Ransom-Kehler, an American citizen, a member of the Bahá'í community of this country, and a distinguished student of the teachings and history of the Bahá'í Faith, can, with your Majesty's gracious permission, amplify and supplement the statements made by this Assembly in the written petition addressed to your Majesty, the Shah, under the date of January 12, 1932.

KEITH enters carrying one small suitcase. She stands centre-stage.

> The appointment of a representative to journey to Tehran for the purpose of presenting in person the petition of this Assembly will make it evident to your Majesty how profoundly the American Bahá'ís are moved by their inability to communicate fully with their fellow-religionists in Persia by reason of the postal regulations still prohibiting the entry of Bahá'í books and magazines published in the United States and Canada.

KEITH: *(moving forward excitedly and interrupting the CHAIR)* Mission successful! On August 15th I saw a Minister of the Crown and received from him the direct, unqualified assurance that Bahá'í literature would be admitted freely into Persia and permitted to be published as well!

But she becomes a little bewildered, her joy fading too quickly as the CHAIRMAN delivers the response.

CHAIRMAN: On behalf of the American Bahá'ís we express abiding gratitude for the removal of the ban on the entry of Bahá'í literature into Persia. This noble action of His Imperial Majesty's Government has profoundly impressed Bahá'ís of the United States and Canada who feel a strong attachment to Bahá'u'lláh's native land. We wish to assure your Highness of our sympathy for his Imperial Majesty, our great interest in the progress and welfare of his Empire and our desire to assist in enhancing its prestige throughout the world.

The AIDE hands the CHAIRMAN a cable. He reads it.

KEITH: *(interrupting)* My books have been confiscated. The meetings arranged among the local believers have been banned. The Minister refuses to see me.

CHAIRMAN: But he had agreed to let the books in.

KEITH: He'd agreed.

CHAIRMAN: Why has he now confiscated them?

KEITH: I don't know!

CHAIRMAN: She must go to see him again.

KEITH: I'll go to see him again.

KEITH picks up her suitcase and rushes off. Meanwhile, the AIDE comes in with another cable which she hands to the CHAIRMAN. KEITH rushes back on again.

KEITH: The Minister definitely will not see me.

CHAIRMAN: Why not?

KEITH: I don't think he's there anymore.

CHAIRMAN: Not there? Why not? Where has he gone?

KEITH: Where have they taken him?

CHAIRMAN: *(horrified)* Have they taken him?

KEITH: He's probably been taken to a certain walled building outside the city where people suspected of disloyalty to the regime are summarily relieved of the burden of existence via a so-called remedial shot.

The actor playing the CHAIR puts on a Panama hat and walks across the front of the stage in front of KEITH. As she notices him, she stops him.

KEITH: Excuse me, sir.

AMBASSADOR: Yes, ma'am? How can I help?

KEITH: Is this the American Embassy?

AMBASSADOR: Yes, it is. You seem to be a little distressed. How can I be of assistance?

KEITH: I'd like to see Ambassador, please.

AMBASSADOR: You are speaking to him. Now, how can I help you today, ma'am?

KEITH: My purpose of being in Iran is to petition for the ability of the Baháʼí community …

AMBASSADOR: *(interrupting)* Is this about Baháʼís?

KEITH: Why, yes it is.

AMBASSADOR: I'm afraid I don't deal with groups that are opposed to the regime. It's against American policy.

KEITH: *(interrupting)* The Bahá'ís are not opposed to the regime. Quite the opposite. It appears the regime is opposing us.

AMBASSADOR: How many American Bahá'ís are in Iran?

KEITH: Not many – a few … well, just me, really. Sir, I need …

AMBASSADOR: *(interrupting again)* I'm sorry, we can't deal with matters that don't affect our American citizens. Now, good day, ma'am.

He makes to leave. She stops him.

KEITH: *(thinking a personal appeal might help)* Sir, please. I do need your help. I had received the express assurance that my Bahá'í books shipped from Beirut would be permitted to enter Iran, but they have been stopped at the border.

He looks at her blankly.

KEITH: *(changing tack)* But this isn't really about me. A royal minister also said that Bahá'í literature could be published on Persian soil, and this is my purpose – to assist my brethren here to win this assurance. But he has gone back on that promise.

AMBASSADOR: *(incredulous)* He gave you a promise? Ma'am, Bahá'í literature cannot circulate in Iran because it is contrary to the constitution of Persia to recognise any religion founded after Islam and it is contrary to the constitution to permit the circulation of literature opposed to Islam. The circulation of Bahá'í literature may also cause internal disorders, affecting suffering to the Bahá'ís themselves. I therefore suggest, ma'am, that you drop this matter immediately. Good day.

He exits quickly. A table and chair are brought on stage left. The AIDE takes out a writing set / pen and paper and sits down to write.

KEITH: *(to the AIDE)* Are you ready? Alright. *(dictating)* Dear Reza Shah. Uh, no, better make that, Your Majesty. No, Your Honoured and Respected Majesty. Yes, OK. I am constrained to admit that I must have misunderstood completely the purpose and intent of the interpreter during my interview with Taymur Tash, for exhaustive investigation reveals no reference in the constitution of Persia to the status of religions founded later than Islam. *(turning to the scribe)* Did you get that? Right.

Since every Baháʼí must accept the validity of the Prophet Muhammad … and since this attitude in inculcated through Baháʼí literature, the point of excluding it because it is opposed to Islam will, I fear, be incomprehensible … *(turning again to the scribe)* How are you doing? OK.

I shall await your Majesty's authority to submit my report to America, for I have no desire, a second time, to find myself mistaken as to your Majesty's intention.

She peers out at the audience questioningly, awaiting an answer. She is confused.

KEITH: No reply *(pause)* … OK – here's another one. Now keep up, won't you? Your Excellency, I appeal for justice. In a land of such ancient beauty and splendour, surely you will also understand justice. The Baháʼís, I must stress, once again, have never worked against Islam or the state, but have always, and I reiterate always championed the principle, no, insert fundamental principle, of loyalty to government, as well as the sanctity of Islam.

KEITH peers out again in silence into the darkness of the audience waiting.

KEITH: No response. Let's write again. *(she is becoming more impatient and fierce)* Dear Shah, may I remind your Majesty again of the Baháʼí community's recognition of your support for religious freedoms in this sacred land, of your lofty accomplishments in that regard in the recent past and, once again, of the utter loyalty of the rank and file of the followers of Baháʼu'lláh in this country to their government? Baháʼí literature, as I have explained in many previous communications, supports Islam.

KEITH looks again out into the audience, waiting and expecting a response. Silence.

KEITH: Nothing. Let's write again …

She mimes continuing to dictate while the CHAIR speaks.

CHAIRMAN: Meanwhile, The Crown issued edicts against the Bahá'ís, removing their previously granted civil rights, and the press virulently attacked the Faith. Conditions became worse than ever for them. Occasional pogroms were augmented by consistent, state-supported discrimination ...

An image of burning is projected onto the screen.

KEITH: *(interrupting, with outrage)* To my horror and grief I have just heard of the burning, on the part of your Majesty's officials in Kirmanshah, of the sacred photographs of 'Abdu'l-Bahá. The Bahá'ís of the world as a body are willing to endure any degree of injustice and persecution themselves, but when it comes to regarding with anything other than outraged sentiment a gratuitous indignity offered to that illustrious example of human perfection, 'Abdu'l-Bahá, they will arise in the full strength of their solidarity to utter a vehement protest.

The MULLAH enters the stage quietly from the rear. He is amused at the display he has witnessed in KEITH. He begins to clap slowly, sarcastically. He comes forward, standing close to her, obviously trying to intimidate her, but KEITH stands straight and strong. He is a little surprised. He hands her a letter casually. She reads it.

KEITH: *(reading aloud)* "Communication from the Minister of Education to Mrs Ransom-Kehler. All inhabitants of Iran, regardless of nationality or conviction, enjoy tranquillity and security under the rule of the Shah. However, new publications considered contrary to the official religion of the country cannot be permitted." *(crying and weaker than before)* But these publications are not contrary to Islam ... Iran's glory is dependant on allowing these books to circulate. If only you could see ...

MULLAH: Where do you come from?

KEITH: America.

MULLAH: America. Is it a Christian country?

KEITH: Yes, you know it is.

MULLAH: And how long did you live in America, Mrs Kehler?

KEITH: I was born there 56 years ago.

MULLAH: 56 years. And in all that time, did you ever come across the Bible, Mrs Kehler?

KEITH: Of course I did! Do you take me for a fool?

MULLAH: (*he laughs*) Now something I don't understand, Mrs Kehler, is how in all that time in a Christian country, surrounded by Christian people, good people believing in God and His Holy Word, the simple fact of the true existence of the Book of God still managed to pass you by? What I find hard to believe is that with every opportunity to embrace this Holy Book, albeit in a previous chapter, you still continue to renounce it for a much inferior false word, which rebukes God and works against Him in the most sinister way. You ask me do I take you for a fool, Mrs Kehler, and the answer would have to be 'Yes, I do'.

KEITH: You don't know what you're talking about. The Bahá'í Writings uphold the truth of …

MULLAH: (*interrupting*) Enough! I have heard enough of this talk. That would be bad enough, but then you come here – to the Stronghold of the Truth of the Word of God Himself – and you try to peddle your poison. You try to turn our own people against God Himself. How dare you, Mrs Kehler! How dare you try to infiltrate the pure blood of Shi'a muslims with the cancer of another doctrine! You bring darkness to our enlightened people.

KEITH: I wrote to the Shah explaining the position of the Bahá'ís. He has ignored me seven times. How can a sovereign worth anything …

MULLAH: He never read your letters.

KEITH: How do you know?

MULLAH: Because the man can't read.

KEITH: You will never deter me from what I believe is the Truth brought by Bahá'u'lláh in this age …

MULLAH: Do not speak his name to me. If you fail your own soul in recognising what is the open and manifest Truth, that is your business, but you may and will not misguide anyone else with your filthy, poisonous literature. At least not in my country.

He grabs the letter roughly and exits swiftly. She coughs and bows her head in weakness, tries to gather herself, and struggles across the stage. Meanwhile, the IRANIAN GOVERNMENT OFFICIAL has taken a seat and has his feet on the table. KEITH approaches.

KEITH: Good afternoon. Is this the Department of Religious Affairs? My name is Keith Ransom-Kehler. I've got an appointment with the attaché.

The OFFICIAL remains 'polite' but condescending in his attitude throughout.

OFFICIAL: Yes, madam. How can I help you today?

KEITH: I need to talk to you about the situation of the Bahá'í's.

OFFICIAL: Oh, madam, this is not the office you need to speak to regarding this matter …

KEITH: Is this not the Department of Religious Affairs?

OFFICIAL: Yes, it is.

KEITH: Well, I need to talk to you about a religious affair …

OFFICIAL: But we don't deal with complaints involving foreigners. *(over-apologetically)* Sorry.

KEITH: But it is not about me – it's about my Persian brethren.

OFFICIAL: Are you involved in any way?

KEITH: Not really.

OFFICIAL: Then why are you here?

KEITH: Well, I'm involved only in their defence.

OFFICIAL: Then you are involved. And we don't deal with complaints involving foreigners.

KEITH: Who can help me?

OFFICIAL: The Department of Foreign Affairs will help you.

They change places – the IRANIAN GOVERNMENT OFFICIAL standing and KEITH in front of the chair.

KEITH: Excuse me, is this the Department of Foreign Affairs?

OFFICIAL: Yes, it is.

He motions for her to sit.

KEITH: I need to speak with the Minister about the case of the Baháʼís not being allowed to freely practise their religion or their literature to freely circulate.

OFFICIAL: *(interrupting)* Oh, I'm sorry, madam. We can't help you with that.

KEITH: Why not? I was told to come to you.

OFFICIAL: I'm not sure why – as this involves a religious minority of Iran itself, so we can't deal with it.

KEITH: I need to speak with someone who will help me … us.

OFFICIAL: I'm sorry, madam, the office is now closed.

KEITH: Closed? But it's 11 o'clock in the morning, and I've just walked in – how can you be closed?

OFFICIAL: *(clearly making it up)* It is a special day today and we close early.

KEITH: I know of no special holiday …

OFFICIAL: I'm so sorry, madam, we cannot help you today. Come back tomorrow.

He exits. The light on KEITH becomes cold as she collapses onto the table. Images of a woman drowning and forget-me-nots float on the screen behind. Then the moving image of the Guardian.

KEITH: Neither am I well. I suffer from sciatica. Up to now, it has been tolerable, but of recent days, I have been suffering from a nerve pain in my back that is very sharp. The pain is so bad I haven't eaten properly for weeks. But the kind face of Shoghi Effendi appears before me daily, gently urging me on. It is my only refuge.

Through this bitter storm of trial in which every attribute of light is obscured or withdrawn, he still stands, a dazzling presence on the further shore towards which I struggle …

A young PERSIAN GIRL dressed in a hijab rushes in happily, grabbing KEITH's hand, pulling her up, and dancing with her, laughing. KEITH recovers her strength. Joyful Persian music plays.

PERSIAN GIRL: Mrs Kehler, you are so loved in Iran. You are the fulfilment of the prophecy of 'Abdu'l-Bahá that brothers and sisters from the West would come to promote the Cause in Iran. You are so beautiful, dear Keith! We will support your work here with our dying breath. Every day we thank God that He has brought you here to be among us, lowly as we are! Are you strong enough to go to the bazaar?

KEITH: Yes! Come! Let's go to the bazaar to see my friends!

KEITH and the PERSIAN GIRL take off excitedly.

KEITH: (*miming meeting the vendors*) Oh! Ahmad! You look so well today. I know you have been under the weather, but today, you just look radiant. What fresh vegetables do you have from the fields?

Sohrab! It is so good to see you – and how is lovely Shohreh? When is her birthday? Next week! I will return with a gift for her which you must promise not to forget to give to the little angel.

Minoo – last week you were so helpful to me with my shopping. So I will buy twice as much from you today!

PERSIAN GIRL: (*pulling KEITH centre-stage and down to sit intimately together on the ground*) Tell us a story, tell us a story!

KEITH: (*laughing happily*) It wasn't until I came to Iran that I heard a real nightingale sing. Now every time I read those words, "Lo! The Nightingale of Paradise singeth upon the twigs of the Tree of Eternity," I know what it really means! But, the welcoming chorus of men's voices singing as I near a Bahá'í village is sweeter to me than any nightingale's song! The Bahá'ís toss flowers in my path, and when I turn the road I see a group of school children singing for me too. Women carry brass trays loaded with fruit, perfume, flowers and incense.

They sprinkle me with rose water and fling fragrant spices before me. In the midst of all this beauty, it is their faces I find the most beautiful …

The PERSIAN GIRL begins to slowly walk backwards and off the stage, reaching out to KEITH.

PERSIAN GIRL: Thank you for saving us, dear Keith. Thank you for saving us.

KEITH sits alone in a cold spotlight. Silence.

KEITH: How strange the ways of God, that I, a poor, feeble, old woman from the West, should be pleading for liberty and justice in the land of Bahá'u'lláh Himself …

Spotlight snaps up on the CHAIR. Throughout the speech, KEITH struggles to her feet, trying to stand with strength.

CHAIRMAN: Resolved! Firstly, the delegates of the 25th American Annual Convention, realising the burdens of oppression still laid upon their Bahá'í brethren of Persia, urge the National Spiritual Assembly to take immediate action to bring about the cessation of their reported maltreatment. Secondly, we also request the Assembly to secure the entry of Bahá'í literature and to restore the constitutional provision for the printing and circulation of Bahá'í literature within Persia.

CHAIRMAN: Request petition again. Stop.

KEITH: But I have already done so … so many times.

CHAIRMAN: Must not withhold any effort. Stop.

KEITH: Any effort.

CHAIRMAN: Beg you try all possible means. Stop.

KEITH: All possible means.

She walks forward into a cold spot.

KEITH: Petition unanswered. Letters unread. No response. Silence. Emptiness. Pain. Weakness. Defeat.

She weakens, as if going to fall. The PERSIAN GIRL rushes on with a chair, gently easing her into it, before kneeling down at KEITH's feet.

PERSIAN GIRL: Tell me a story.

KEITH: One day a knight, prepared for battle and saying his last goodbyes to his lady, is walking with her by a river. The valiant and passionate knight, wishing to show his love for his lover, spots a small bunch of blue flowers down by the bank. His armour is heavy and with great difficulty bends down to pick the flowers from the riverside. But this action causes him to topple over into the river, the weight of his armour pulling him down deep into the water. His loved one stands helpless on the bank, calling out and crying. The knight, with his last breath throws the posy of flowers he picked to his lover and calls out, "Forget me not!" *(to the PERSIAN GIRL, reassuring her)* I'm alright. I'm fine. Really.

KEITH sends the PERSIAN GIRL away.

I have fallen, and am drowning, though I never faltered. Months of effort with nothing accomplished is the record that confronts me, defeated, the battle lost. If anyone in future should be interested in this thwarted adventure of mine, he alone can say whether near or far from the seemingly impregnable heights of complaisance and indifference my tired old body fell, dragged down into the river by the weight of the task. The smoke and din of the battle are today too dense for me to ascertain whether I moved forward or was slain in my tracks. The river has at last overwhelmed me.

(weeping) Nothing in this world is meaningless, suffering least of all. Sacrifice with its attendant agony is a germ, an organism. Man cannot blight its fruition as he can the seeds of earth. Once sown it blooms, I think forever, in the sweet fields of eternity. Mine will be a very modest flower, perhaps like the single, tiny forget-me-not, watered by the blood of Quddús that I plucked from his graveside in Bárfurúsh; should it ever catch the eye, may one who seems to be struggling in vain garner it in the name of Shoghi Effendi and cherish it for his dear remembrance.

It's time for me to leave Iran. Maybe I'll return to India now. Or perhaps beloved Shoghi Effendi still wants me to go to Europe …

A spotlight rises on the PERSIAN GIRL. She is holding a wrapped-up white sheet like a baby. She is crying and the sound of a baby crying is heard.

KEITH: What's wrong?

PERSIAN GIRL: It is the child.

KEITH: What is wrong with the child?

The PERSIAN GIRL only weeps.

KEITH: (*struggling up and walking over to comfort the girl*) Shhh, it's alright. Everything will be alright. Do you not think that God knows what is best for us? He is watching us now. He is protecting us. (*pause*) Let me hold the child.

PERSIAN GIRL: No! You cannot! She is not healthy.

KEITH: It's alright (*she laughs wryly*), neither am I.

PERSIAN GIRL: No – you do not want it. She has smallpox. You will catch it.

KEITH: (*pause*) I too had a baby once. Please, please, let me hold her … just once more.

The PERSIAN GIRL gently passes the baby to KEITH, who holds it so tenderly. KEITH unfurls the sheet, laying it on the floor and disappears off stage. The PERSIAN GIRL weeps. She arranges the sheet into a 'grave'. 'Flowers' are handed to the CHAIRMAN. These are made using the sari, the red silk kimono and the black lace worn on her travels, folded to look decorative.

CHAIRMAN: (*walking over to the grave carrying the 'flowers'*) In accordance with the wishes of the Guardian, the Bahá'ís made a pilgrimage to Keith's grave. The cemetery was a desolate spot near Isfahan – dusty, rocky ground with flat stones lying over the graves, a line of jagged mountains beyond. The mourners covered Keith's grave with desert flowers.

The PERSIAN GIRL mimes sprinkling water. The CHAIRMAN lays the 'flowers' on the grave.

CHAIRMAN: One of the Bahá'ís sprinkled it with rosewater from the house of the Báb in Shiraz. They placed a large photograph of her on the grave wreathed with flowers.

The photograph appears on the screen.

CHAIRMAN: This photograph had been taken in Tehran only a few months before. Keith was beautifully dressed, facing the camera with elegant posture and a bright if somewhat tremulous smile. Just before the photo was taken, Keith had been weeping over the failure of her mission; she had held back the tears for the photographer.

Music swells. A message, sent by Shoghi Effendi, is projected, phrase by phrase on the screen. The CHAIRMAN stands behind the PERSIAN GIRL, who kneels at the graveside.

'Keith's precious life offered up in sacrifice to beloved Cause in Bahá'u'lláh's native land. On Persian soil, for Persia's sake, she encountered, challenged and fought the forces of darkness with high distinction, indomitable will, unswerving, exemplary loyalty. The mass of her helpless Persian brethren mourns the sudden loss of their valiant emancipator. American believers grateful and proud of the memory of their first and distinguished martyr. Sorrow stricken, I lament my earthly separation from an invaluable collaborator, an unfailing counsellor, an esteemed and faithful friend … one whose international services entitled her to an eminent rank among the Hands of the Cause of Bahá'u'lláh.

– SHOGHI EFFENDI RABBANI

Her picture returns and is held for a few minutes then fades with the music to silence. Blackout.

THE END

www.ingramcontent.com/pod-product-compliance
Ingram Content Group UK Ltd.
Pitfield, Milton Keynes, MK11 3LW, UK
UKHW050522150426
5217IPUK00026B/1755